CELEBRATING THE NAME LINDA

Celebrating the Name Linda

Walter the Educator

Silent King Books a WhichHead Imprint

Copyright © 2024 by Walter the Educator

All rights reserved. No part of this book may be reproduced in any manner whatsoever without written permission except in the case of brief quotations embodied in critical articles and reviews.

First Printing, 2024

Disclaimer
This book is a literary work; poems are not about specific persons, locations, situations, and/or circumstances unless mentioned in a historical context. This book is for entertainment and informational purposes only. The author and publisher offer this information without warranties expressed or implied. No matter the grounds, neither the author nor the publisher will be accountable for any losses, injuries, or other damages caused by the reader's use of this book. The use of this book acknowledges an understanding and acceptance of this disclaimer.

dedicated to everyone with the first
name of Linda

CONTENTS

Dedication v

One - Here's To Linda 1

Two - Linda's Presence 3

Three - Purest Gold 5

Four - Linda, Oh Linda 7

Five - Dances On The Breeze 9

Six - Everlasting Mark 11

Seven - Elegance And Grace 13

Eight - Indelible Mark 15

Nine - A Valentine 17

Ten - Every Letter 19

Eleven - Cherished Forevermore 21

Twelve - Linda, So Fine 23

Thirteen - Soaring High 25

Fourteen - Beautiful Gifts 27

Fifteen - Gem So Rare 29

Sixteen - Melody Of Joy 31

Seventeen - Artisan Of Language 33

Eighteen - Harmonious Anthem 35

Nineteen - Everlasting Grace 37

Twenty - Cosmic Rhyme 39

Twenty-One - Poetic Heartbeat 41

Twenty-Two - Lyrical Delight 43

Twenty-Three - A Whisper 45

Twenty-Four - Radiant Light 47

Twenty-Five - Name Of Measure 49

Twenty-Six - Linda Blooms 51

Twenty-Seven - Linda Takes The Stage 53

Twenty-Eight - Universe Unfurls 55

Twenty-Nine - Anthem Of Beauty 57

Thirty - Peaceful Night 59

Thirty-One - Divinely Spun 61

Thirty-Two - Harmonious Stroll 63

Thirty-Three - Flower Of Kindness 65

Thirty-Four - Celestial Light 67

About The Creator 69

ONE

HERE'S TO LINDA

 Linda, oh lustrous name of grace,
A melody that time can't erase,
In every syllable, a story untold,
A name that shines like purest gold.
 In gardens fair, where lilies bloom,
The name of Linda casts out gloom,
A gentle breeze, a soothing song,
That carries hearts where they belong.
 In valleys deep and mountains high,
Linda's name echoes through the sky,
A beacon of hope, a guiding light,
That banishes darkness, brings forth delight.
 In ancient tales and legends spun,
Linda's name, a prize to be won,
A symbol of strength, a spirit bold,
A legacy that shall never grow old.

In the dance of stars and ocean's swell,
Linda's name, a magic spell,
Enchanting souls with its gentle power,
A name that blooms like a fragrant flower.
So here's to Linda, a name so grand,
A jewel in the world's vast land,
In every letter, a tale to unfold,
A name of wonder, a sight to behold.

TWO

LINDA'S PRESENCE

    Linda, a name like a symphony in the breeze,
A gentle whisper that sways the trees,
In every letter, a world of wonder,
A name that echoes like distant thunder.
    In fields of emerald and skies of sapphire,
Linda's name, a beacon of fire,
A radiant glow, a celestial spark,
That lights up the universe, even in the dark.
    In the tapestry of time, a name so divine,
Linda's essence, like aged wine,
A richness of spirit, a depth of soul,
A name that weaves together, making us whole.
    In the dance of life, a name that leads,
Linda's presence, a garden of seeds,
A blossoming hope, a flourishing dream,
A name that glistens in every sunbeam.

In the symphony of words, a name that sings,
Linda's melody, an anthem that rings,
A harmony of grace, a rhythm so true,
A name that paints the sky in a vibrant hue.
So here's to Linda, a name so rare,
A treasure to cherish, beyond compare,
In every breath, a story to unfold,
A name that shimmers like molten gold.

THREE

PUREST GOLD

Linda, a name that dances on the wind,
A symphony of letters, beautifully pinned,
In each syllable, a universe unfurls,
A name that shines, like precious pearls.

In meadows lush and forests deep,
Linda's name, a promise to keep,
A gentle melody, a soothing rhyme,
That lingers on through endless time.

In the tapestry of fate and chance,
Linda's name, a graceful dance,
A whisper of hope, a touch of grace,
That fills the world with an enchanting embrace.

In the mosaic of life, a name that gleams,
Linda's essence, a river of dreams,
A beacon of light, a guiding star,
That leads the way, no matter how far.

In the gallery of art and song,
Linda's name, a masterpiece long,
A stroke of genius, a stroke of love,
That paints the sky and soars above.

So here's to Linda, a name so bright,
A symphony of joy, a radiant light,
In every verse, a tale to be told,
A name that sparkles like purest gold.

FOUR

LINDA, OH LINDA

Linda, oh Linda, with a name so divine
Like a rare gem, in a world full of shine
Your name dances on the lips, a melody so sweet
A symphony of letters, in perfect, graceful fleet
In the garden of names, yours blooms like a rose
A timeless beauty, that everyone knows
It whispers in the wind, and echoes in the air
A name so enchanting, beyond all compare
Linda, oh Linda, with a name so profound
It carries a history, a story that's unbound
In every syllable, a tale untold
Of strength and grace, a sight to behold
Like the sunrise, painting the sky with its hue
Your name shines bright, in all that you do
In every letter, a spark of light
Guiding the way, through day and night

    Linda, oh Linda, with a name so pure
In a world of noise, it stands secure
A name that resonates, in hearts far and near
A symphony of love, that we all hold dear

FIVE

DANCES ON THE BREEZE

    Linda, a name that sparkles like dew at dawn
A symphony of syllables, a name to fawn
In every letter, a universe unfurls
A name that glows, and endlessly twirls
    In the tapestry of names, yours is a masterpiece
A name that echoes, and will never cease
In every sound, a melody takes flight
A name that shimmers, in the darkest night
    Linda, oh Linda, with a name so rare
It carries a legacy, beyond compare
In every whisper, a tale is spun
Of triumphs and trials, of battles won
    Like a lighthouse, guiding ships in a storm
Your name stands tall, in its graceful form

In every verse, a story is told
Of passion and poise, of courage bold
    Linda, a name that dances on the breeze
A name that soothes, and puts hearts at ease
In every moment, it rings out loud
A name that stands out, in a bustling crowd

SIX

EVERLASTING MARK

    Linda, oh Linda, a name that gleams and glows
In the garden of names, it elegantly grows
Like a melody, it dances on the tongue
A name that feels like a sweet, unsung song
    In every letter, a story unfolds
Of strength and kindness, worth more than gold
Linda, a name that carries such grace
A beacon of hope in life's bustling race
    In the tapestry of names, it stands out bold
A name that shines, a treasure to behold
In every syllable, a legacy resides
Of resilience and love that fiercely abides
    Linda, oh Linda, with a name so divine
In every echo, a radiant shine
Like a diamond, it sparkles and gleams
A name that embodies hopes and dreams

In every whisper, it paints a new tale
Of compassion and warmth that will never pale
Linda, a name that lights up the dark
A name that leaves an everlasting mark

SEVEN

ELEGANCE AND GRACE

Linda, oh Linda, a name that sings with grace
In the symphony of names, it finds its place
Like a gentle breeze, it whispers in the air
A name that carries stories, beyond compare
In every letter, a journey unfolds
Of resilience and courage, in tales untold
Linda, a name that embodies strength
A beacon of hope, through any length
In the tapestry of names, it stands out bright
A name that radiates warmth and light
In every syllable, a legacy lives on
Of love and kindness, from dusk till dawn
Linda, oh Linda, with a name so pure
In every verse, its beauty will endure

Like a rare gem, it sparkles and gleams
A name that weaves through hopes and dreams
    In every whisper, it paints a new story
Of compassion and joy, in all its glory
Linda, a name that leaves a lasting trace
A name that embodies elegance and grace

EIGHT

INDELIBLE MARK

Linda, oh Linda, a name that blooms with might
In the garden of names, it shines so bright
Like a symphony, it dances in the wind
A name that holds secrets, waiting to be pinned
In every letter, a tale takes flight
Of resilience and hope, through the darkest night
Linda, a name that echoes through time
A beacon of strength, in its graceful climb
In the tapestry of names, it stands tall and true
A name that resonates, in all that you do
In every syllable, a story is weaved
Of love and compassion, never to be deceived
Linda, oh Linda, with a name so divine
In every echo, a radiant shine
Like a precious jewel, it sparkles with grace
A name that reflects kindness, in every embrace

In every whisper, it paints a new saga
Of courage and wisdom, like an ancient saga
Linda, a name that leaves an indelible mark
A name that ignites hope, even in the dark

NINE

A VALENTINE

Linda, a name so sweet and kind,
In every heart, she leaves a shine,
With grace and charm, she walks the line,
Her presence, like a rare vintage wine.
  In fields of flowers, she finds her peace,
Her laughter, like a soothing breeze,
In every soul, she plants a seed,
Of hope and joy, she takes the lead.
  Linda, a name that echoes love,
A gift to earth from skies above,
In every word, a melody, a dove,
Her essence, a symphony, a treasure trove.
  In every step, she paints a tale,
Of resilience, courage, without fail,
With kindness as her holy grail,
In every heart, she leaves a trail.

Linda, a name that shines so bright,
In every darkness, a guiding light,
With every hug, a warm delight,
Her presence, a beacon in the night.

In every smile, a universe unfolds,
In every dream, her spirit holds,
Linda, a name that never grows old,
In every story, a legend untold.

Linda, a name that's truly divine,
In every soul, a sacred shrine,
With every moment, a new design,
Her name, a symphony, a valentine.

TEN

EVERY LETTER

    Linda, oh Linda, with a name so divine
Like a melody, your name does shine
In a world of chaos, you bring peace
Your name brings joy, it will never cease
    Linda, the name that echoes through the ages
In every line, in every page, it's been etched for ages
A name that whispers of grace and strength
A name that carries the weight of a thousand dreams at length
    In the garden of names, yours is a blooming rose
A name that in every letter, beauty it shows
L is for the love you bring to all you meet
I is for the inspiration you make so sweet
N is for the nurturing nature you possess
D is for the dignity in which you dress
A is for the amazing aura you emanate

    Linda, your name is a symphony of elegance
A tapestry of grace, woven with resilience
In every syllable, a story unfolds
Of a woman so bold, a name so untold
    So here's to Linda, a name like no other
A name that embodies strength and power
Linda, oh Linda, may your name forever ring
In the hearts of those who love and sing

ELEVEN

CHERISHED FOREVERMORE

Linda, oh how your name doth sing,
Like a melody from a celestial spring.
In every letter, a story unfolds,
A tale of grace that never grows old.

L is for the light you bring into the day,
Illuminating hearts along the way.
N is for the nurturing nature you possess,
A gentle touch to calm and bless.

D is for the dreams you dare to chase,
Inspiring others to find their own unique space.
A is for the artistry that flows from your soul,
Creating beauty that makes the world whole.

Linda, your name is a symphony of sound,
A harmonious blend that echoes all around.

In every syllable, a universe unfurls,
A name that dances and spins and twirls.
   So here's to you, Linda, so kind and rare,
A name that carries a spirit beyond compare.
May it be celebrated and cherished forevermore,
For the essence of Linda is one to adore.

TWELVE

LINDA, SO FINE

    Linda, oh how your name brings a melody,
A symphony of sounds that dances merrily.
In every letter, a story to be told,
In every syllable, a beauty to behold.
    L is for the love you spread with grace,
I is for the intelligence that lights up your face,
N is for the nurturing nature you possess,
D is for the delightful spirit you express,
A is for the abundance of kindness you share.
    Oh Linda, your name is a precious gem,
A beacon of hope in a world so dim.
It resonates like a gentle breeze,
Whispering tales of strength and ease.
    In every consonant and vowel, a tale unfolds,
Of a woman so bold, with a heart of gold.

Linda, your name is a work of art,
A masterpiece of love, right from the start.
    So let's raise a toast to Linda so dear,
Her name like music to the ear.
May it always shine bright and true,
Just like the wonderful person that is you.
    Linda, oh how your name inspires,
A symphony of joy, it never tires.
So here's to you, dear Linda, so fine,
In your name, a world of wonders entwine.

THIRTEEN

SOARING HIGH

Linda, a name that blossoms like a garden in spring,
A tapestry of sounds that make the heart sing.
In each letter, a tale of resilience and might,
In each syllable, a spark that ignites the night.
Luscious L, for the laughter you bring,
Infectious and genuine, like the first days of spring.
Incredible I, for the intellect that guides your way,
A beacon of wisdom, brightening every day.
Noble N, for the nurturing soul you possess,
A comforting presence, a haven in distress.
Dazzling D, for the dreams you dare to chase,
A fearless spirit, leaving a trail of grace.
Adored A, for the affection you freely share,
A boundless love that shows how much you care.
Linda, your name is a melody of hope,
A symphony of strength to help us cope.

It echoes through the valleys and over the hills,
A name that resonates, a cure for all ills.
    In every consonant and vowel, a story blooms,
Of a woman so vibrant, breaking all glooms.
Linda, your name is a treasure to behold,
A testament to love, more precious than gold.
    So let's raise a glass to Linda so dear,
Her name a symphony for all to hear.
May it always shine, radiant and true,
Just like the wonderful person that is you.
    Linda, your name ignites the sky,
A beacon of hope, soaring high.

FOURTEEN

BEAUTIFUL GIFTS

Linda, a name that dances on the wind,
A symphony of letters that paints a vivid blend.
In every letter, a tale of joy and grace,
In every syllable, a portrait of strength and embrace.
L is for the laughter that fills the air,
I is for the inspiration you effortlessly share,
N is for the nurturing spirit within,
D is for the determination that helps you win,
A is for the affection that knows no end.
Oh Linda, your name is a melody so sweet,
A harmonious rhythm, a delightful feat.
It resonates like a gentle lullaby,
Bringing comfort and warmth to the sky.
In every consonant and vowel, a story unfolds,
Of a woman so resilient, with a heart of gold.

Linda, your name is a masterpiece divine,
A reflection of love that continues to shine.
    So let's raise a toast to Linda so true,
Her name a symphony, a vibrant hue.
May it always echo through the universe wide,
Just like the extraordinary person by its side.
    Linda, your name is a beacon so bright,
Guiding us through the darkest night.
A name that inspires, a name that uplifts,
A name that encompasses all the beautiful gifts.

FIFTEEN

GEM SO RARE

Linda, oh Linda, your name sings a sweet melody,
A symphony of grace and strength, a sight to see,
In fields of flowers, your name blooms like a lily,
A name so lovely, it dances in the wind so freely.
Linda, a name that shines like the morning sun,
A name that whispers of adventures to be spun,
In the tapestry of life, your name weaves a tale,
Of courage and kindness that will never pale.
Linda, your name is a beacon in the darkest night,
Guiding lost souls with its gentle light,
In the echoes of the mountains, your name reverberates,
A name that carries the weight of countless fates.
Linda, a name that holds the power of the ocean's tide,
A name that stands tall, never trying to hide,

In the vast expanse of the universe, your name soars,
A name that opens a thousand different doors.
    Linda, oh Linda, your name is a work of art,
A masterpiece that captivates every heart,
In the symphony of names, yours stands out,
A name that we will always talk about.
    Linda, your name is a treasure, a gem so rare,
A name that fills the world with love and care,
In every language, your name is a beautiful sound,
A name that makes the earth's very foundation astound.

SIXTEEN

MELODY OF JOY

Linda, the name that dances on the breeze,
A melody of joy, a whisper in the trees,
In the garden of names, yours blooms with grace,
A name that paints a smile on every face.

Linda, a name that sparkles like the morning dew,
A name that holds the promise of skies so blue,
In the story of life, your name is the guiding light,
A name that fills the world with pure delight.

Linda, your name is a symphony of elegance and might,
A name that conquers the darkness, shining so bright,
In the tapestry of dreams, your name weaves a tale,
A name that will forever prevail.

Linda, a name that echoes through the ages,
A name that adorns history's endless pages,

In the vast expanse of time, your name stands strong,
A name that will forever belong.
 Linda, oh Linda, your name is a precious gem,
A name that outshines every diadem,
In every heart, your name finds a place,
A name that fills the world with love and grace.
 Linda, your name is a symphony, a dance, a song,
A name that will forever carry on,
In the tapestry of existence, your name is a precious thread,
A name that we will never cease to tread.

SEVENTEEN

ARTISAN OF LANGUAGE

In realms of reverie, where echoes dance,
Linda, a name, a lyrical romance.
A melody sung by zephyrs so sweet,
In the tapestry of existence, a heartbeat.
    Lustrous as moonbeams, a celestial glow,
Linda, the empress of dreams doth bestow.
Each syllable, a sonnet in the night,
Whispered by stars, adorned in delight.
    Amidst the meadows where wildflowers bloom,
Linda's essence, a fragrant perfume.
Her name, a voyage on the river of time,
Echoing verses in a poetic climb.
    In the gallery of words, she takes her place,
A masterpiece painted with eloquent grace.

A kaleidoscope of hues, vivid and grand,
Linda, the artisan of language, takes a stand.
   Through the echoes of ages, her name shall soar,
A phoenix of letters, forevermore.
Unique in the symphony of linguistic art,
Linda, the muse, plays an eternal part.

EIGHTEEN

HARMONIOUS ANTHEM

In the tapestry of nomenclature, a gem so rare,
Linda, a symphony, beyond compare.
Bathed in the radiance of celestial light,
Her name weaves tales, a poetic flight.
Lustrous as dawn's first kiss on the sea,
Linda, the oracle of linguistic glee.
A sonnet sung by the quills of time,
Her name dances in rhythm, a sublime.
Blossoming in gardens where words entwine,
Linda's resonance, a vintage wine.
Her syllables paint an aurora in the mind,
A kaleidoscope of thoughts, intertwined.
Among the constellations of lexicon's embrace,
Linda, a comet, leaves an indelible trace.

In the mosaic of language, she's the prime,
A linguistic ballet, a paradigm.
    Through the verses, she's an eternal flame,
Linda, the maestro in the lexicon game.
Her name, a crescendo in the literary choir,
A harmonious anthem that will never tire.

NINETEEN

EVERLASTING GRACE

In the realm of whispers, where syllables bloom,
Linda, a melody in the lexicon's loom.
Her name, a sonnet spun by cosmic hands,
An eloquent dance in linguistic sands.
Radiant as the dawn's ethereal glow,
Linda, a serenade, a luminous show.
Her essence, a fragrance in the poetic air,
A timeless sonnet beyond compare.
Beneath the moon's tender, silvery grace,
Linda, a poem adorned with grace.
Her syllables cascade like a river's flow,
A lyrical ballet in the meadow.
In the tapestry of language, she weaves,
Linda, the poetess, who eternally believes.
Her name, a phoenix in the literary fire,
A symphony that continues to inspire.

Among the constellations of verses untold,
Linda, a narrative of silver and gold.
Her presence, an ode to the celestial sphere,
A celestial ballad that we hold dear.

Through the corridors of time, she strides,
Linda, where eloquence and beauty abides.
Her name, an anthem in the language's embrace,
A poetic journey, an everlasting grace.

TWENTY

COSMIC RHYME

In the garden of lexicon, a bloom named Linda,
A linguistic enchantress, her aura tender.
Her name, a melody in the moonlit night,
A sonnet written in the stars' soft light.

Lustrous as dew on petals at dawn,
Linda, a lyric, a celestial spawn.
Her syllables dance like butterflies,
A poetic symphony that never denies.

Beneath the tapestry of language, she shines,
Linda, where eloquence sweetly twines.
Her essence, an echo in the poet's quill,
A serenade that time cannot distill.

In the gallery of verses, she's a masterpiece,
Linda, a mural where words find release.
Her name, a canvas painted with hues,
A poetic odyssey that forever renews.

Through the labyrinth of prose, she weaves,
Linda, the storyteller who eternally believes.
Her syllables, like whispers in the breeze,
A literary dance that effortlessly appease.
Among the constellations of metaphorical art,
Linda, a constellation, a work of heart.
Her presence, a verse in the cosmic rhyme,
A poetic journey that transcends space and time.

TWENTY-ONE

POETIC HEARTBEAT

In a realm where echoes of laughter intertwine,
Linda, a name like a melody divine.
Blossoming in syllables, a lyrical dance,
Graceful and timeless, a linguistic romance.
　　Her name, a whisper in the zephyr's embrace,
A symphony of letters, each with its own grace.
Lustrous as moonbeams on a tranquil night,
Linda, a constellation in language's light.
　　Amidst the lexicon, she stands bold and free,
A linguistic tapestry woven seamlessly.
Vowels and consonants in harmonious array,
Linda, a sonnet, a poetic display.
　　In the garden of words, she blooms with flair,
Petals of prose, delicate and rare.
A serenade of syllables, a cadence so sweet,
Linda, the poetic heartbeat.

As the quill dances on the parchment's stage,
Her name pirouettes in an eloquent page.
A kaleidoscope of linguistic hues,
Linda, the lyric, forever muse.
　　Oh, Linda, in the lexicon's ballet,
Your name pirouettes, a linguistic array.
A celebration in verses, uniquely spun,
In the tapestry of words, forever to be sung.

TWENTY-TWO

LYRICAL DELIGHT

    In the tapestry of language, a portrait is drawn,
Linda, a beacon, with words uniquely dawned.
A symphony of syllables, a linguistic ballet,
Her name, a sonnet, in the poetic array.
    Linda, the echo of laughter in every verse,
A linguistic universe where sentiments immerse.
In the lexicon's garden, her name blooms,
A kaleidoscope of letters, language resumes.
    Like a celestial melody in the cosmic choir,
Linda, a celestial spark, ignites the fire.
With consonants and vowels, a dance profound,
In the realm of words, her name is crowned.
    Embodied in prose, a lyrical delight,
Linda, a phoenix in the language's flight.
Sculpted in syllables, each one a gem,
Her name, a sonnet, a linguistic diadem.

A linguistic voyage, a poetic spree,
Linda, a verse that sets the spirit free.
In the anthology of names, she stands unique,
A symphony of sounds, a linguistic mystique.
Oh, Linda, in the lexicon's grand ballet,
Your name pirouettes in the poetic display.
A celebration in verses, a literary song,
In the realm of words, you forever belong.

TWENTY-THREE

A WHISPER

In the tapestry of language, behold the grace,
Linda, a melody that time can't erase.
With syllables like petals in a linguistic bloom,
Her name, a whisper, in the lexicon's room.
A symphony of letters, a dance divine,
Linda, in the verses, forever shall shine.
In the mosaic of words, a radiant hue,
Her name, a sonnet, both vibrant and true.
Embraced by consonants, kissed by vowels sweet,
Linda, in the linguistic garden, takes her seat.
A poetic phoenix, in language she soars,
Each syllable, a canvas, where beauty explores.
In the sonnet of names, a ballad unique,
Linda, the verses in which emotions peak.
A dance of letters, a rhythmic spree,
Her name, a lyrical voyage, wild and free.

Oh, Linda, in the lexicon's grand array,
Your name, a serenade, in the linguistic ballet.
With every utterance, a tale unfolds,
In the realm of words, a narrative molds.

So let the verses weave their enchanting spell,
Linda, in the poetry, forever dwell.
A symphony of sounds, a linguistic art,
In the grand mosaic, you play a central part.

TWENTY-FOUR

RADIANT LIGHT

In the cosmic realm of words, a star is born,
Linda, a name adorned, in language sworn.
With syllables like stardust, a celestial ballet,
Her name, a constellation, lighting the way.
    Linda, a serenade in the poet's quill,
A linguistic sonnet, a tranquil thrill.
In the tapestry of language, a masterpiece,
Her name, a lyrical symphony, it won't cease.
    Each letter a brushstroke, painting the air,
Linda, a masterpiece, beyond compare.
Vowels and consonants waltz in harmony,
In the gallery of words, a name to see.
    Embraced by verses, a poetic embrace,
Linda, a muse, in the linguistic space.
A sonnet woven with threads of grace,
Her name, an elegy, in the lyrical chase.

In the lexicon's garden, a rare blossom,
Linda, a name, sweet as spring's awesome.
Sculpted in syllables, a linguistic dance,
In the manuscript of poetry, a cherished trance.
Oh, Linda, in the poetry's grand array,
Your name, a journey in the linguistic play.
A celebration in verses, unique and bright,
In the cosmos of words, a radiant light.

TWENTY-FIVE

NAME OF MEASURE

In the gallery of language, a portrait unfolds,
Linda, a masterpiece, in stories untold.
With syllables dancing, a linguistic ballet,
Her name, a sonnet, in the poetic array.

Linda, a melody on the lips of the breeze,
A cadence of letters that gracefully tease.
In the tapestry of words, a radiant thread,
Her name, an ode, where emotions are bred.

Each consonant and vowel, a brushstroke divine,
Linda, a painting where words intertwine.
In the sonnet of verses, a symphony rings,
Her name, a serenade, as the poet sings.

A poetic canvas, her name takes its place,
Linda, a muse, in the language's embrace.
Sculpted in syllables, a linguistic dance,
In the poetic sanctuary, she enchants.

Oh, Linda, in the lexicon's grand design,
Your name, a beacon, in the literary shrine.
A celebration in verses, unique and bright,
In the gallery of words, a radiant light.

In the tapestry of time, her name weaves,
Linda, a poetic legacy that eternally leaves
An imprint on verses, a linguistic treasure,
In the anthology of names, a name of measure.

TWENTY-SIX

LINDA BLOOMS

In the realm of echoes, where names dance in poetic grace,
Linda emerges, a melody woven with celestial lace.
A symphony of syllables, a serenade in letters,
Her name, a sonnet, each verse a gift that fetters.
  L is for the lustrous light she brings,
I is the ink of inspiration her presence sings.
N, the notes of her laughter, a sweet refrain,
D, the dawn breaking, dispelling every pain.
  In the garden of language, Linda blooms,
Petals of prose, a fragrant spell that consumes.
Her name, a voyage through realms unknown,
A tapestry of words, a linguistic throne.
  From the quill of imagination, her essence unfurls,
In the lexicon of uniqueness, she whirls.

A kaleidoscope of vowels and consonants,
Linda, a language's vibrant resonance.
    Oh, Linda, in the mosaic of letters you reside,
A lexical masterpiece, in which you preside.
In the anthology of names, a jewel so rare,
Your symphonic resonance fills the poetic air.

TWENTY-SEVEN

LINDA TAKES THE STAGE

In the cosmic ballet of appellations, Linda takes the stage,
A ballet of syllables, a linguistic sage.
With the brush of words, painting her name,
A masterpiece in letters, a linguistic flame.

Luscious Linda, a lexicon's delight,
In the garden of language, she takes flight.
Each consonant and vowel, a poetic dance,
Her name, an eloquent sonnet's trance.

Luminous as the moonlight, Linda beams,
A celestial sonata in the realm of dreams.
Draped in the garments of linguistic art,
Her name, a canvas where words impart.

Lingering on lips, a mellifluous sound,

In the symphony of names, Linda is crowned.
Dancing through verses, a lyrical sprite,
Her name, a constellation in the poetic night.
    Labyrinth of letters, where her essence weaves,
In the tapestry of expression, Linda conceives.
A linguistic alchemy, a magical brew,
Her name, a potion that words imbue.
    Oh, Linda, in the lexicon's embrace,
A poetic journey, an endless chase.
With every word, a tribute to your fame,
Linda, the protagonist in this linguistic game.

TWENTY-EIGHT

UNIVERSE UNFURLS

In the realm of language, where symphonies unfold,
Linda, a melody, a tale untold.
A linguistic phoenix, rising from the prose,
Her name, a voyage where expression flows.
   Lustrous Linda, a luminary of letters,
In the tapestry of words, she's what matters.
Each syllable, a star in her cosmic trail,
Her name, a celestial wind in language's sail.
   In the lexicon's garden, she gracefully treads,
Petals of phrases bloom where Linda spreads.
A linguistic ballet, a poetic trance,
Her name, a rhythmic echo, a rhythmic dance.
   Lingering on lips, like honeyed wine,
In the mosaic of sounds, her name will shine.
Draped in verses, a lyrical attire,
Linda, the flame in language's fire.

Labyrinth of expressions, where she roams,
In the sonnet of names, Linda composes.
A poetic odyssey, an endless rhyme,
Her name, a timeless, linguistic chime.
Oh, Linda, in the lexicon's embrace,
A muse for words, a celestial space.
With every syllable, a universe unfurls,
Linda, the poetess of linguistic pearls.

TWENTY-NINE

ANTHEM OF BEAUTY

In the realm of nomenclature, a star shines bright,
Linda, a name that graces with celestial light.
In the vast expanse of linguistic delight,
It unfolds, a symphony, a melodious flight.

    Linda, a word that dances with gentle grace,
A sonnet whispered, an eternal embrace.
Derived from Spanish roots, a blossom fair,
It blooms in hearts, a fragrant affair.

    Meaning, a tapestry woven with delicate thread,
Linda, the cherished, where love is bred.
A moniker that echoes through the ages,
An anthem of beauty, as history engages.

    In the lexicon, it holds a sacred space,
Linda, a reflection of elegance and grace.

A compass pointing to realms of kindness,
A name that transcends the boundaries of blindness.
   Celebrate Linda, in verses, let it sing,
A name that's timeless, a perennial spring.
In the mosaic of existence, it stands,
Linda, a masterpiece, painted by skilled hands.

THIRTY

PEACEFUL NIGHT

In the realm of names, a melody unfolds,
Linda, a symphony, a tale yet to be told.
A name that dances on the lips with grace,
In its essence, a beauty, an eternal embrace.
    Linda, derived from the Spanish, a tender flower,
Blooming in hearts, wielding gentle power.
A name that whispers in the winds of time,
Resonating love, a rhythm so sublime.
    In the etymology, a meaning profound,
Linda, the cherished, the world around.
It signifies beauty, both inside and out,
A beacon of kindness, dispelling any doubt.
    In the tapestry of existence, Linda weaves,
A name that perseveres, like autumn leaves.
Harmonizing with the universe's grand design,
Linda, a constellation in the cosmic sign.

Celebrate this name, a beacon of light,
In every sunrise, in the peaceful night.
Linda, a symphony, a poetic refrain,
In the lexicon of life, an everlasting gain.

THIRTY-ONE

DIVINELY SPUN

In the realm of names, a gem shines bright,
Linda, a melody that brings delight.
A name adorned with grace and charm,
A symphony of letters, a soothing balm.
　L, the luminous beacon of her name,
Guiding hearts with a gentle flame.
Illuminating paths with kindness and care,
Linda, a name beyond compare.
　N, the nurturing spirit she holds,
A garden of love, where beauty unfolds.
D, the dance of dreams in her gaze,
A poetic journey through life's maze.
　A name that echoes in the winds of time,
Linda, a harmonious paradigm.
In every syllable, a tale untold,
A story of warmth and virtues bold.

Oh, Linda, in the tapestry of existence,
Your name weaves threads of sweet persistence.
A melody sung by the cosmic choir,
A name that sets hearts afire.
Celebrate Linda, a symphony of sound,
In the universe's grand playground.
A name, a masterpiece, divinely spun,
In the gallery of life, forever to be sung.

THIRTY-TWO

HARMONIOUS STROLL

In the tapestry of nomenclature, a star does gleam,
Linda, a name that sparks a radiant dream.
A symphony of letters, gracefully entwined,
In the garden of language, a bloom defined.

L, the lustrous beginning, a beacon of light,
Leading through realms, day and night.
In the lexicon of grace, Linda takes flight,
A celestial dance in the moon's soft light.

I, an echo of individuality and grace,
A unique charm in the name's embrace.
Linda, a melody, a poetic trace,
In the heart's ballad, finding its space.

N, the nurturing whispers of the soul,
In Linda's embrace, kindness takes its toll.
A name that resonates, an anthem's role,
In the symposium of life, a harmonious stroll.

D, the dance of dreams within her name,
A canvas painted with aspirations aflame.
Linda, a portrait in the language frame,
A masterpiece in the etymology game.
So, celebrate Linda, in prose and rhyme,
A moniker adorned with beauty sublime.
In the vast lexicon, a gem to chime,
Linda, a name that withstands the test of time.

THIRTY-THREE

FLOWER OF KINDNESS

In the realm of names, a melody unfolds,
Linda, a symphony of stories yet untold.
A name that dances in the moonlit night,
A beacon of grace, an ethereal light.
    Linda, oh, what secrets do you bear,
In your letters, whispers of love in the air.
Meaning woven into the fabric of time,
A tapestry of dreams, a poetic rhyme.
    L, for the laughter that echoes in your name,
I, for the infinite joy you effortlessly claim.
N, for the nurturing spirit you possess,
D, for the dance of life, a sweet caress.
    In the garden of existence, you bloom,
A flower of kindness, chasing away gloom.
Linda, a canvas painted with hues so rare,
A masterpiece of compassion beyond compare.

Your name, a river flowing with tranquility,
Carving paths of serenity with gentle ability.
In the tapestry of existence, a thread divine,
Linda, a name that forever will shine.

THIRTY-FOUR

CELESTIAL LIGHT

In the grand lexicon of life, a gem shines bright,
Linda, a name draped in celestial light.
In the symphony of syllables, you stand,
A melody of grace, like a whispering strand.
Linda, oh, what tales do your letters tell?
In the alphabetic dance, a magical spell.
L, a lantern illuminating laughter's path,
I, an echo of joy that escapes love's hearth.
N, the note of nurture in your embrace,
D, a dance in every step, full of grace.
A name, not mere letters strung together,
But a poetic narrative that lasts forever.
In the garden of meanings, you blossom,
Linda, a bloom dispelling life's gloom.
Your name, a tapestry woven with care,
A canvas painted with hues rare.

L, the lullaby sung by the moon,
I, the ink in a lover's swoon.
N, the navigator of dreams untold,
D, the dance of time in stories old.
Linda, a symphony, a sonnet divine,
A name that in every heartbeat will shine.
In the lexicon of existence, you're the art,
Linda, a masterpiece, a beat in every heart.

ABOUT THE CREATOR

Walter the Educator is one of the pseudonyms for Walter Anderson. Formally educated in Chemistry, Business, and Education, he is an educator, an author, a diverse entrepreneur, and he is the son of a disabled war veteran. "Walter the Educator" shares his time between educating and creating. He holds interests and owns several creative projects that entertain, enlighten, enhance, and educate, hoping to inspire and motivate you.

Follow, find new works, and stay up to date with Walter the Educator™ at WaltertheEducator.com

www.ingramcontent.com/pod-product-compliance
Lightning Source LLC
LaVergne TN
LVHW010604070526
838199LV00063BA/5071